ESTES ADESIVOS COMPÕEM O *THE FRUIT AND VEGETABLE GAME* (JOGO DAS FRUTAS E DOS VEGETAIS) E DEVEM SER COLADOS NA CAPA DO LIVRO PARA FORMAR SEQUÊNCIAS.

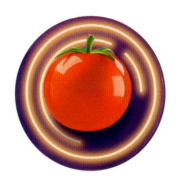

CB027981

ELIETE CANESI MORINO • RITA BRUGIN DE FARIA

Hello!

KINDER 3

EDUCAÇÃO INFANTIL

editora ática

CONTENTS

ACOMPANHA ESTE LIVRO O *READER* **BOB, THE FROG**.

ICONS

 CIRCLE

 COLOR

 COUNT

 CUT

 DOT TO DOT

 DRAW

 GLUE

 INTERNET

 LET'S TALK

 LISTEN AND SAY

 MAKE AN X

 MATCH

 NUMBER

 POINT

 PRINT

 SING OR CHANT

 STICK

GROWING UP

LET'S TALK!

SING AND CIRCLE.

BE POLITE!

wong sze yuen/Shutterstock

Ideário Lab/Arquivo da editora

UNIT 1 AT SCHOOL

STUDENT

BOOK

WELCOME, STUDENTS!

SCHOOLBAG

TEACHER

ERASER

PENCIL

7

LISTEN AND CIRCLE.

MATCH.

CIRCLE THE ODD ONES.

1

2

3

4

Savanevich Viktar/Shutterstock

Alexandra Ribeiro / EyeEm/ Getty Images

PicsNew/Alamy/Fotoarena

tanuha2001/Shutterstock

Ilustrações: Ideário Lab/Arquivo da editora

9

GROWING UP

LET'S TALK!

SING AND DRAW.

PAY ATTENTION!

LISTEN AND COLOR.

1 RED

2 YELLOW

3 BLUE

4 GREEN

5 ORANGE

6 PINK

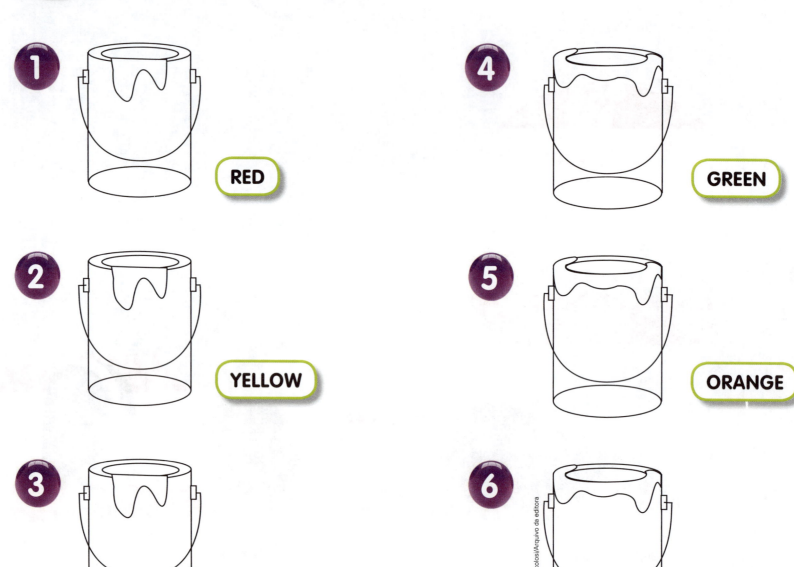

Ilustrações: Ari Nicolosi/Arquivo da editora

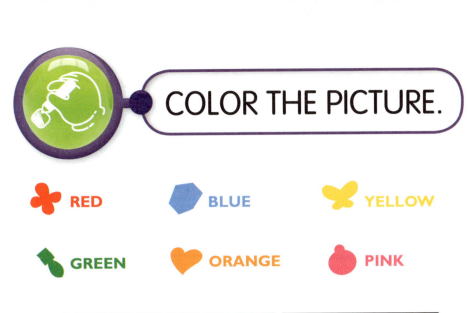

COLOR THE PICTURE.

🔴 **RED**   🔷 **BLUE**   🦋 **YELLOW**

🟢 **GREEN**   💛 **ORANGE**   🔴 **PINK**

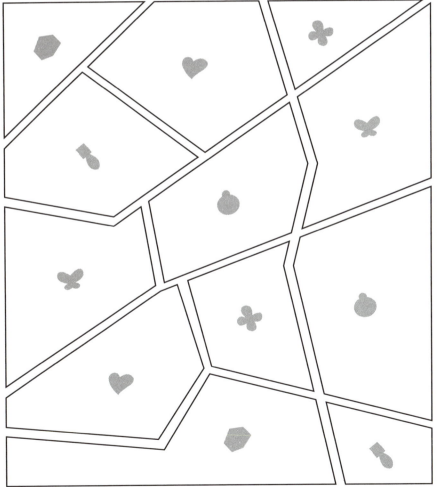

STICK.

Ilustrações: Ari Nicolosi/Arquivo da editora

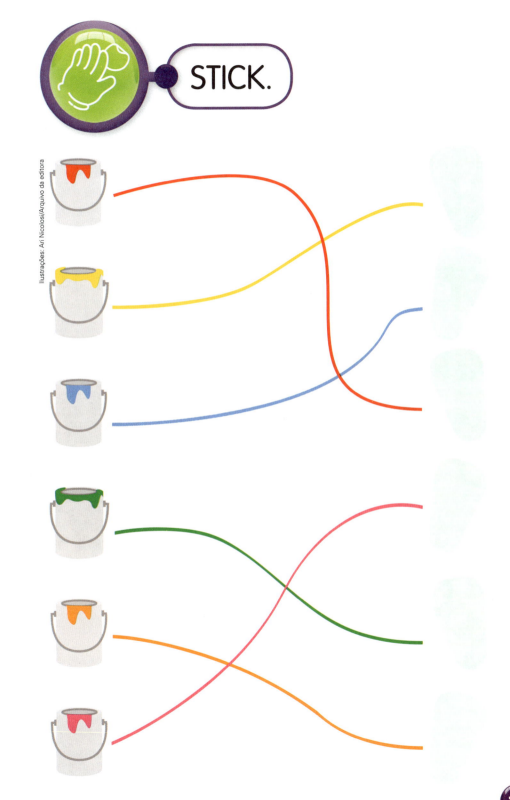

GROWING UP

LET'S TALK!

SING AND MATCH.

GOOD SOCIALIZATION RULES!

LET'S COUNT!

ONE

TWO

THREE

FOUR

FIVE

SIX

SEVEN

EIGHT

NINE

TEN

Aline Sentone/Arquivo da editora

LISTEN, DOT TO DOT AND COLOR.

1.

.3

7.

5

8.

.6

10.

.4

2

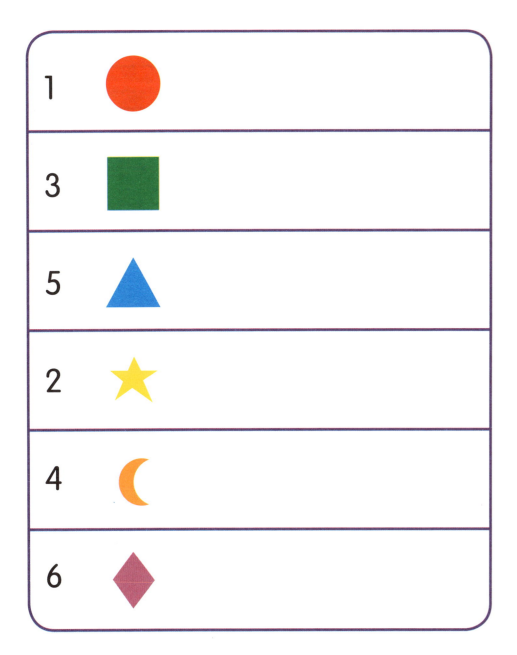

1 🔴

3 🟩

5 🔺

2 ⭐

4 🌙

6 ◆

Dan Kosmayer/Shutterstock

Fotocrisis/Shutterstock

Audrius Merfeldas/Shutterstock

stable/Shutterstock

Physicx/Shutterstock

8

9

10

6

7

GROWING UP

LET'S TALK!

OBEY THE RULES!

Fernando Favoretto/Criar Imagem

SING AND STICK.

Ideário Lab/Arquivo da editora

4 AT THE GYM CLASS

SWIMMING

SOCCER

GYMNASTICS

JUDO

TUG OF WAR

Aline Sentone/Arquivo da editora

19

LISTEN AND NUMBER.

MATCH.

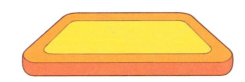

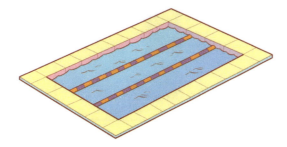

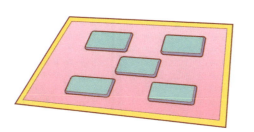

COUNT.

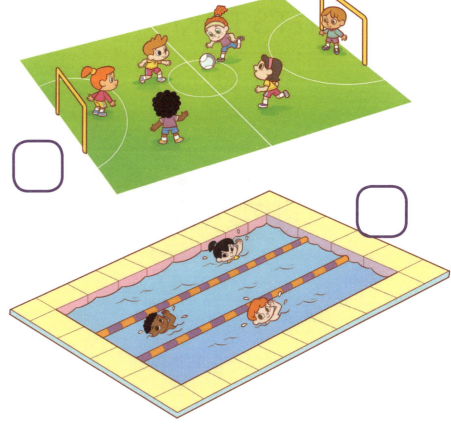

Ilustrações: Idério Lab/Arquivo da editora

GROWING UP

LET'S TALK!

SING AND CIRCLE.

EXERCISING IS IMPORTANT!

Christopher Futcher/Getty Images

stockyimages/Shutterstock

Jeka/Shutterstock

LumineImages/Shutterstock

ISSARET YATSOMBOON/Shutterstock

Samuel Borges Photography/Shutterstock

CIRCLE.

Ideário Lab/Arquivo da editora

MATCH AND COMPLETE THE JIGSAW.

CIRCLE 5 DIFFERENCES.

GROWING UP

LET'S TALK!

FOLLOW THE RULES!

SING AND COLOR.

HOME SWEET HOME

KITCHEN

BATHROOM

LIVING ROOM

BEDROOM

Aline Sentone/Arquivo da editora

LISTEN AND NUMBER.

 STICK.

 DRAW YOUR BEDROOM.

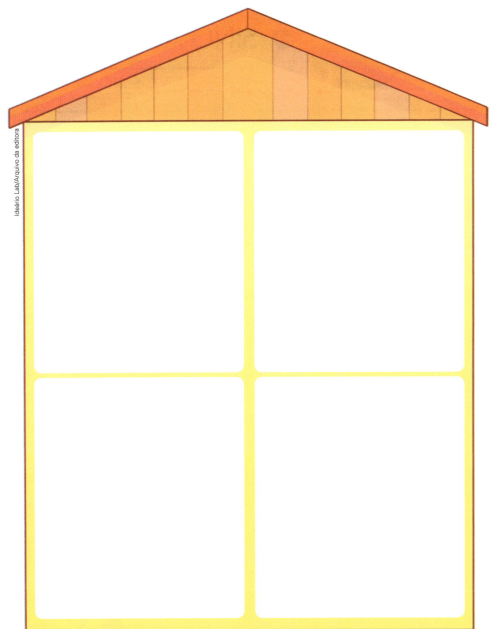

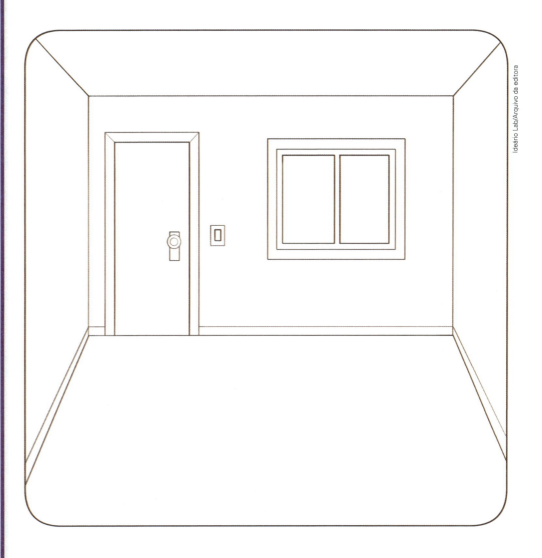

GROWING UP

LET'S TALK!

TIDY UP!

Bob Ebbesen/Alamy/Fotoaren

SING AND COLOR.

Ideário Lab/Arquivo da editora

ORANGE

PAPAYA

APPLE

BANANA

CARROT

LETTUCE

TOMATO

LISTEN AND CIRCLE.

onair/Shutterstock

Valery121283/Shutterstock

Tim UR/Shutterstock

Gavran333/Shutterstock

Roman Samokhin/Shutterstock

Ekaterina Simonova/Shutterstock

MAKE AN X.

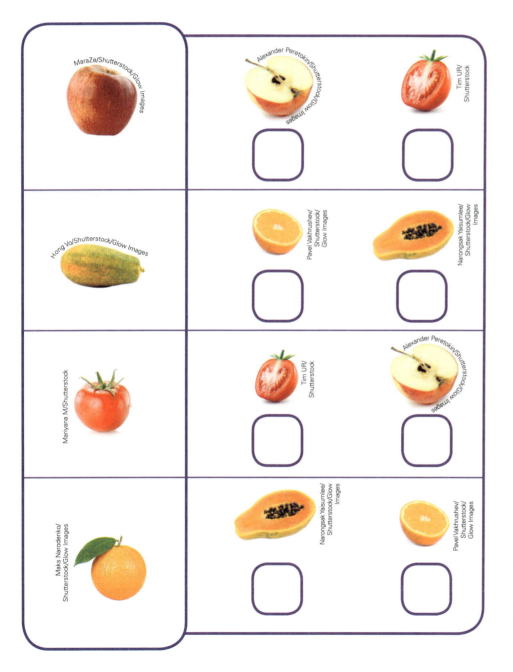

STICK.

LETTUCE

TOMATO

BANANA

APPLE

CARROT

ORANGE

PAPAYA

33

GROWING UP

LET'S TALK!

SING AND COLOR.

HEALTHY EATING HABITS!

Ilike/Shutterstock

Ideário Lab/Arquivo da editora

LISTEN AND MAKE AN X.

incamerastock/ Alamy/Fotoarena

Delfim Martins/ Pulsar Imagens

Filipe Frazao/Shutterstock

Jeff Whyte/Shutterstock

Sorbis/Shutterstock

Sunny Forest/Shutterstock

VGstockstudio/Shutterstock

JMich/Getty Images

paul prescott/Shutterstock

Alinute Silzeviciute/ Shutterstock

Ideário Lab/Arquivo da editora

GROWING UP

LET'S TALK!

SING AND COLOR.

RESPECT!

Africa Studio/Shutterstock

Ideário Lab/Arquivo da editora

38

UNIT 9

WILD ANIMALS

MONKEY

LION

GIRAFFE

ELEPHANT

ALLIGATOR

LISTEN AND STICK.

 MATCH.

 COMPLETE THE PICTURE AND COLOR.

Ilustrações: Ideário Lab/Arquivo da editora

GROWING UP

 LET'S TALK!

 SING AND GLUE.

RESPECT THE ANIMALS!

VP Photo Photo Studio/Shutterstock

LISTEN AND DRAW.

COLOR BY NUMBERS.

Ideário Lab/Arquivo da editora

1. 🟥 **RED**	3. 🟦 **BLUE**	5. 🟧 **ORANGE**
2. 🟨 **YELLOW**	4. 🟫 **BROWN**	6. 🟩 **GREEN**

COMPLETE THE SEQUENCE.

GROWING UP

 LET'S TALK!

 SING AND CIRCLE.

ORGANIZATION!

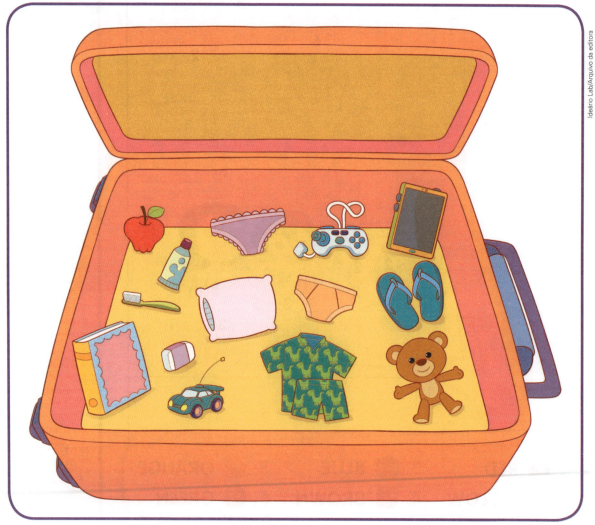

LISTEN AND NUMBER.

Ilustrações: Aline Sentone/Arquivo da editora

Aline Sentone/Arquivo da editora

Ilustrações: Ideário Lab/Arquivo da editora

1

2

3

GROWING UP

LET'S TALK!

SING AND STICK.

PERSONAL HYGIENE!

Svitlana-ua/Shutterstock

Sergey Novikov/Shutterstock

wavebreakmedia/Shutterstock

Chirtsova Natalia /Shutterstock

LISTEN AND MATCH.

Idéario Lab/Arquivo da editora

MAKE AN X.

MATCH THE SCENES.

GROWING UP

LET'S TALK!

RESPONSIBILITY!

SING AND COLOR.

HAPPY BIRTHDAY!

HAPPY BIRTHDAY TO YOU!

HAPPY BIRTHDAY TO YOU,

HAPPY BIRTHDAY TO YOU,

HAPPY BIRTHDAY, DEAR CAROL!

HAPPY BIRTHDAY TO YOU!

KidStock/Blend Images/Getty Images

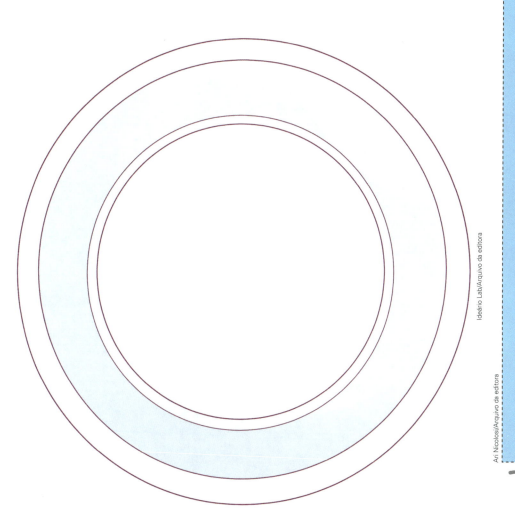

Ideário Lab/Arquivo da editora

Ari Nicolosi/Arquivo da editora

HAPPY EASTER!

EASTER BUNNY

EASTER BUNNY,

EASTER BUNNY,

WHAT DO YOU BRING TO ME?

ONE EGG, TWO EGGS, THREE EGGS, SO, SO!

ONE EGG, TWO EGGS, THREE EGGS, SO, SO!

Africa Studio/Shutterstock

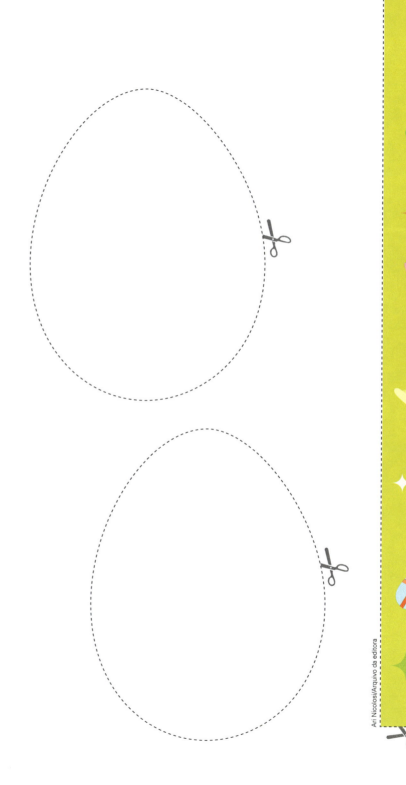

Ari Nicolosi/Arquivo da editora

HAPPY MOTHER'S DAY!

DEAR MOM!

MY MOM, MY LOVE!

SO SWEET, SO SWEET!

MY MOM, MY LOVE!

SO KIND, SO PRETTY!

Evgeny Atamanenko/Shutterstock

Ari Nicolosi/Arquivo da editora

· · · · DOBRE

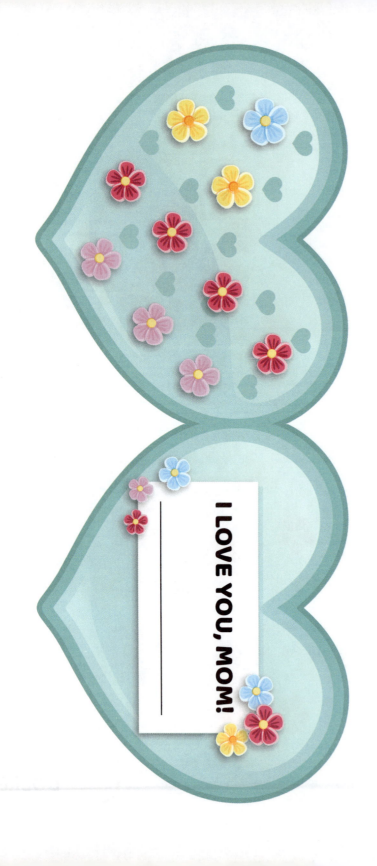

I LOVE YOU, MOM!

HAPPY FATHER'S DAY!

MY DAD

MY DAD IS MY FRIEND

FROM BEGINNING TO END.

MY DAD IS ALL TO ME,

HE IS MORE THAN YOU CAN SEE!

Ariel Skelley/Getty Images

···· DOBRE

DAD, I LOVE YOU!

Banco de imagens/Arquivo da editora

Ari Nicolosi/Arquivo da editora

COLE AQUI

THANKSGIVING DAY

MR. TURKEY

MR. TURKEY, MR. TURKEY,

RUN AWAY, RUN AWAY,

PLEASE, BE CAREFUL!

[…]

IT'S THANKSGIVING DAY!

MERRY CHRISTMAS!

WE WISH YOU A MERRY CHRISTMAS!

WE WISH YOU A MERRY CHRISTMAS,

WE WISH YOU A MERRY CHRISTMAS,

WE WISH YOU A MERRY CHRISTMAS,

AND A HAPPY NEW YEAR!

Monkey Business Images/Shutterstock

Ari Nicolosi/Arquivo da editora

THE SONG BOOK

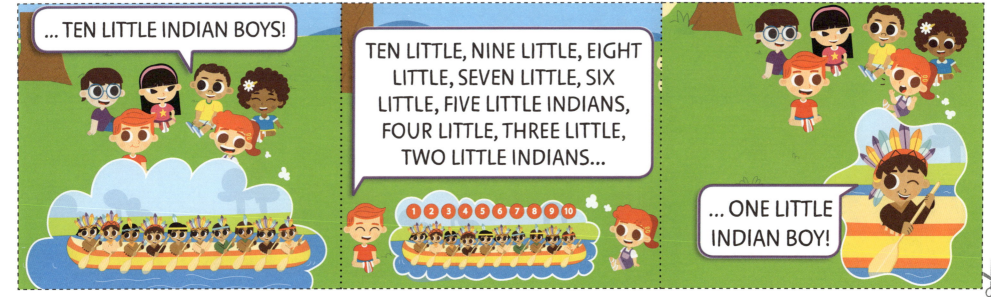

ABA PARA COLAR

THE SONG BOOK
TEN LITTLE INDIANS

PICTURE DICTIONARY

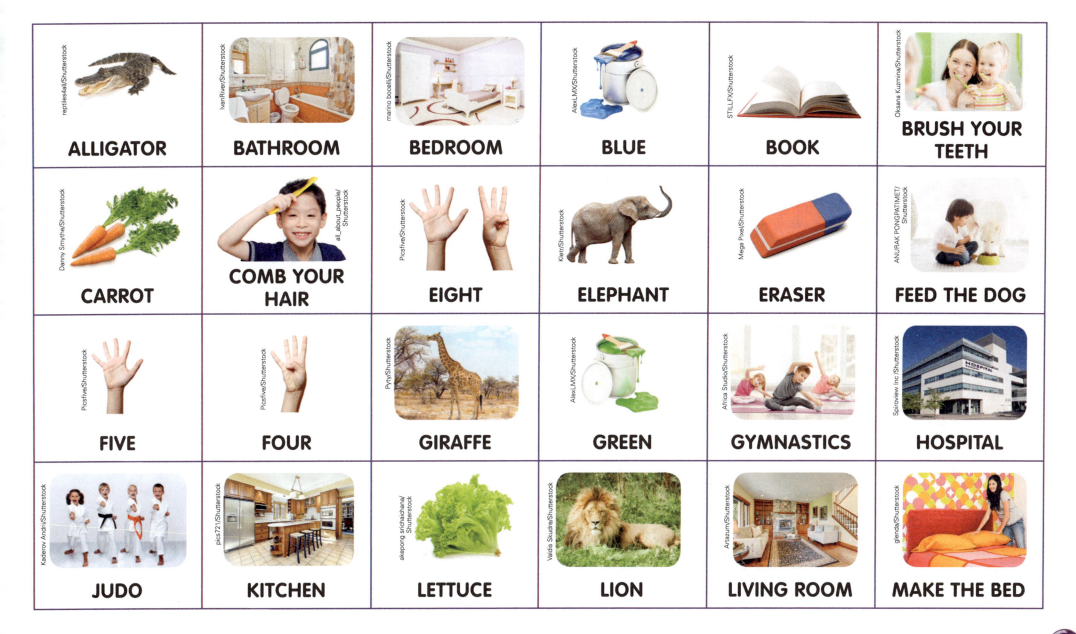

ALLIGATOR	**BATHROOM**	**BEDROOM**	**BLUE**	**BOOK**	**BRUSH YOUR TEETH**
CARROT	**COMB YOUR HAIR**	**EIGHT**	**ELEPHANT**	**ERASER**	**FEED THE DOG**
FIVE	**FOUR**	**GIRAFFE**	**GREEN**	**GYMNASTICS**	**HOSPITAL**
JUDO	**KITCHEN**	**LETTUCE**	**LION**	**LIVING ROOM**	**MAKE THE BED**

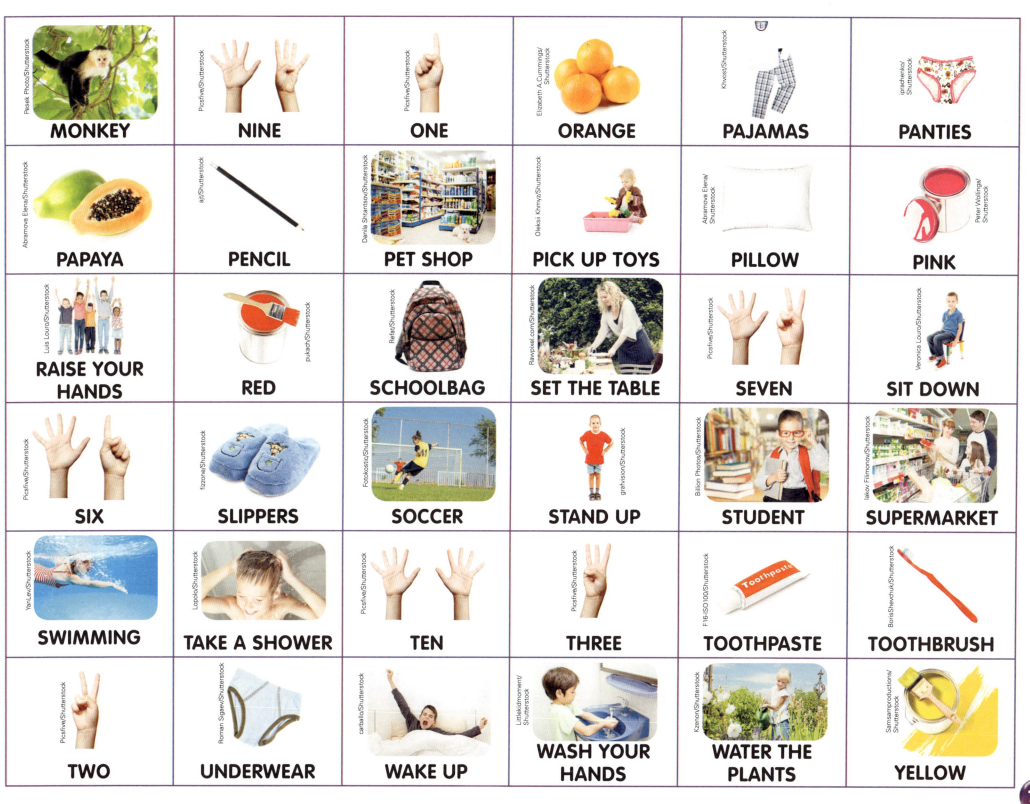

MONKEY	NINE	ONE	ORANGE	PAJAMAS	PANTIES
PAPAYA	PENCIL	PET SHOP	PICK UP TOYS	PILLOW	PINK
RAISE YOUR HANDS	RED	SCHOOLBAG	SET THE TABLE	SEVEN	SIT DOWN
SIX	SLIPPERS	SOCCER	STAND UP	STUDENT	SUPERMARKET
SWIMMING	TAKE A SHOWER	TEN	THREE	TOOTHPASTE	TOOTHBRUSH
TWO	UNDERWEAR	WAKE UP	WASH YOUR HANDS	WATER THE PLANTS	YELLOW

STICKERS

PAGE 6

NAME

NAME

NAME

PAGE 16 - READER

PAGE 13

PAGE 18

1 7 2 10 5

PAGE 29

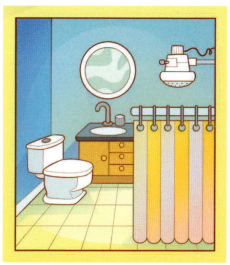 

PAGE 50

PAGE 40

PAGE 33

MEMORY GAME

WAKE UP

WAKE UP

MAKE THE BED

MAKE THE BED

WASH YOUR HANDS

WASH YOUR HANDS

COMB YOUR HAIR

COMB YOUR HAIR

BRUSH YOUR TEETH

BRUSH YOUR TEETH

TAKE A SHOWER

TAKE A SHOWER

NUMBERS GAME

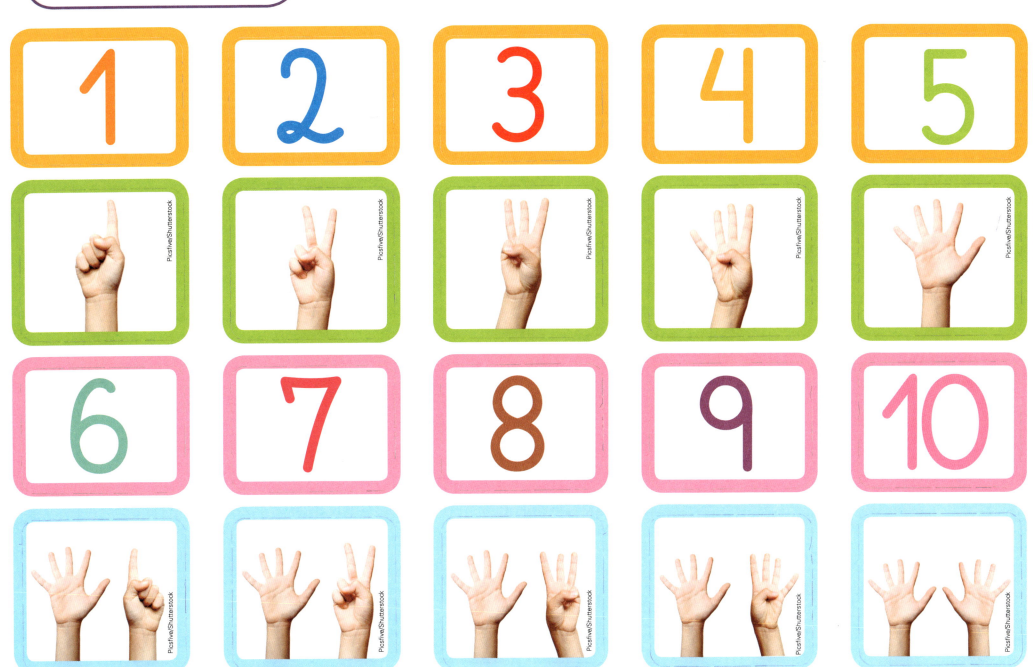

PUPPETS

Ilustrações: Aline Sentone/Arquivo da editora

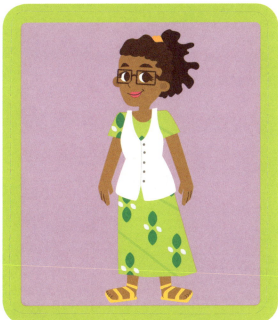

FIDO

HOME, SWEET HOME & YES, I CAN!

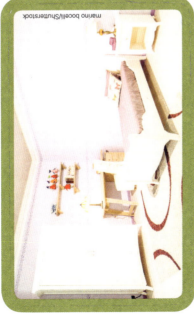

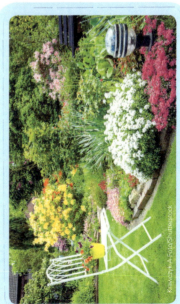

AT SCHOOL & SPORTS

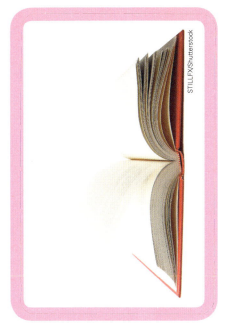

HEALTHY FOOD

akepong srichaichana/Shutterstock

Tim UR/Shutterstock

Danny Smythe/Shutterstock

homydesign/Shutterstock

GMEVIPHOTO/Shutterstock

Tim UR/Shutterstock

Elizabeth A.Cummings/Shutterstock

Abramova Elena/Shutterstock

Tim UR/Shutterstock

LZ Image/Shutterstock

THE CITY & WILD ANIMALS

Pesek Photo/Shutterstoc

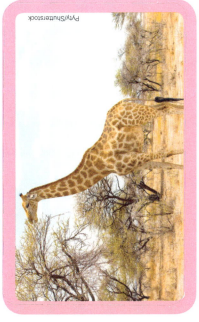
Pyty/Shutterstock

Jakub Skula/Shutterstock

reptiles4all/Shutterstock

Kletr /Shutterstock

Alexey Fillimonov/Shutterstock

Spiroview Inc./Shutterstock

Andersen Ross/Blend Images/Getty Images

s_oleg/Shutterstock

Danila Shtantsov/Shutterstock

PACKING TO VISIT GRANDMA & SIMON SAYS

Luis Louro/Shutterstock

Veronica Louro/Shutterstock

grafvision/Shutterstock

DarkBird/Shutterstock

anythings/Shutterstock

Khvost/Shutterstock

Abramova Elena/Shutterstock

fizkes/Shutterstock

Roman Sigaev/Shutterstock

iprachenko/Shutterstock